On a car journey

INTRODUCTION

If you take i-SPY On a Car Journey with you every trip will be fun for you and the family, no matter how long or short. What's more, you'll have a record of everything you've seen, so you can compare notes with your friends when you get back.

If you're going on a long journey, like from one side of the country to the other, it's worth taking the time and trouble to do a bit of planning. Look at a road atlas and follow the route that you're going to take – then when you're travelling you'll always know which road you're on and exactly where you are. Try to work out how long the journey might take – how far are you travelling and what speed do you think the driver will go?

If you keep your eyes open and look all around you there's so much to see on a car journey. It's fun to find out about the world as it rushes by, and you'll be surprised by all the fascinating things you discover. But, whatever you do, do not distract the driver by pointing things out to him or her, and be sure to wear a seatbelt and make yourself as comfortable as possible.

How to use your i-SPY book

There are so many things you could look out for on a car journey that it's hard to know where to begin, what to include, or what to leave out. Your i-SPY On a Car Journey book aims to give you some ideas but, once you've spotted everything here, why not come up with some more ideas of your own?

You need 1000 points to send off for your i-SPY certificate (see page 64) but that is not too difficult because there are masses of points in every book. Each entry has a star or circle and points value beside it. The stars represent harder to spot entries. As you make each i-SPY, write your score in the circle or star.

If you see these signs, you might be in for a short delay, so look out for some of the excavators and loaders on the next page.

ROADWORKS

5 Points: 5

ROAD AHEAD CLOSED

ROAD
AHEAD
CLOSED

5 Points: 5

WORKS IN TOWN CENTRE

Business
Open
As Usual

5 Points: 5

CONES

To keep workers safe.

5 Points: 5

PRIORITY

5 Points: 5

DIVERSION

Diversion

5 Points: 5

Excavators and rollers rake and flatten the earth to make a smooth surface for a new road.

DIGGING UP THE ROAD

Points: 5
for each type of vehicle

Points: 10

LAYING TARMAC

Then tarmac can be spread to make a hard durable road surface.

4

TRACKED EXCAVATOR

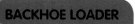 Points: 10

WHEEL LOADER

This one has a big bucket on the front.

Points: 10

BACKHOE LOADER

Points: 10

Note the scoop mounted at the rear.

POLICE

Throughout the country the police will be there, seven days a week and 24 hours a day, to enforce the law or to offer help and advice.

BLUE LAMP

Points: 15

Traditionally, the sign of the police station.

POLICE BOX

Points: 25 **Top Spot!**

Once a common sight on British streets. It is now more common as *Dr Who's* Tardis!

WHEEL CLAMP

Points: 5

Oh dear! This driver will come back to a nasty surprise when he returns to his vehicle.

Driving too fast can be dangerous. These devices help police to measure the speed of passing cars.

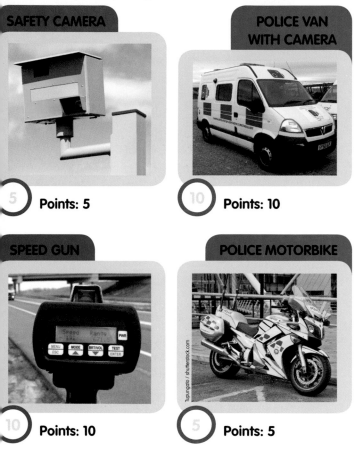

SAFETY CAMERA

5 Points: 5

POLICE VAN WITH CAMERA

10 Points: 10

SPEED GUN

10 Points: 10

POLICE MOTORBIKE

5 Points: 5

7

POLICE VEHICLES

Points: 5
for each of these

5

There are many types of police vehicle currently in use. Here is a selection.

8

If your car breaks down, you might need a roadside recovery vehicle. Recovery trucks are heavy vehicles strong enough to transport smaller cars and trucks.

FIRE ENGINE

Like the police and ambulance services, fire engines have blue flashing lights.

 Points: 10

RECOVERY TRUCK

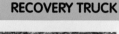

Points: 5

ROADSIDE ASSISTANCE

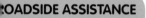 **Points: 5**
and 5 points for any roadside assistance van

CRASH RECOVERY

Points: 10

9

Ambulances have fluorescent strips and blue flashing lights so that they are highly visible on the road.

AMBULANCE

Points: 5

AMBULANCE

Points: 5

Points: 20

AIR AMBULANCE

The air ambulance helicopter can transport crash victims to hospital very quickly.

You'll find different postboxes in most towns and villages. They are often stamped with a date when the postbox was put in place. Postboxes also have the royal cypher of the monarch on them.

TRADITIONAL RED POSTBOX

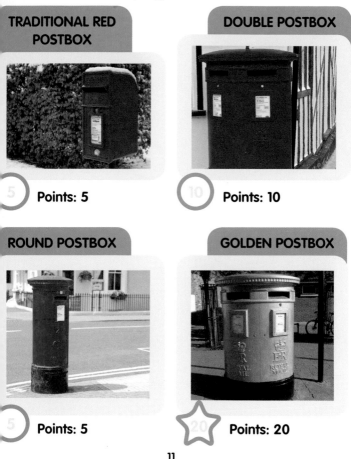

Points: 5

DOUBLE POSTBOX

Points: 10

ROUND POSTBOX

Points: 5

GOLDEN POSTBOX

Points: 20

POST OFFICE

Tupungato / shutterstock.com

Points: 5

POST OFFICE SIGN

Post offices now have lozenge shaped signs.

Points: 5

RED PHONE BOX

Phone boxes are disappearing from our towns.

Points: 5

BLUE PHONE BOX

 Points: 25 Top Spo

The Royal Mail transports millions of letters every day. As well as postmen and women delivering on foot, small vans are used for local collections while articulated lorries move large quantities of post between cities.

5

Points: 5
for each of these

POSTAL VANS

War memorials and statues are erected in honour of famous people and events.

STATUE OF QUEEN VICTORIA

Points: 15

WAR MEMORIAL

Points: 10

14

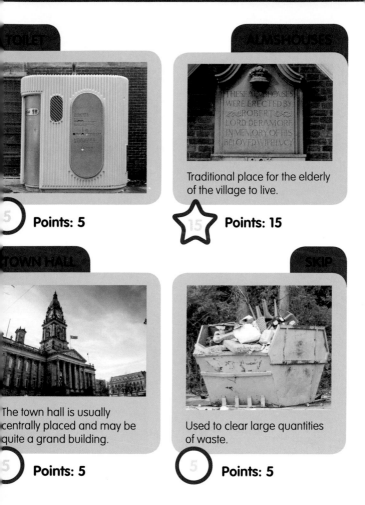

TOILET

Points: 5

ALMSHOUSES

Traditional place for the elderly of the village to live.

Points: 15

TOWN HALL

The town hall is usually centrally placed and may be quite a grand building.

Points: 5

SKIP

Used to clear large quantities of waste.

Points: 5

MARKET

The market brings hustle and bustle to the streets with vendors selling farmers' produce and home-made foods.

Points: 15

ORNAMENTAL FOUNTAIN

Points: 10

PADDLING POOL

Great for hot summer days!

Points: 20

CIRCUS

Points: 25   Top Sp

16

Points: 10
for each flag and 5 for other flags

FLAGS

Can be found outside town halls and other public buildings.

EUROPEAN UNION FLAG

FRENCH FLAG

ITALIAN FLAG

BRITISH FLAG

VILLAGE FAIR

Points: 10

Village fairs are a lot of fun especially in the summer.

Points: 5

PUB GARDEN

Pub gardens are a great place to relax on a fine day with a lemonade.

DUCK POND

Points: 15

Be very careful of the water.

Points: 25 Top Spot!

CHALK MAN

The Cerne Abbas Giant is carved into chalky hillside in southern England.

ANCIENT MONUMENT

Points: 10

There are 1000 stone circles like this in the British Isles.

Points: 25 Top Spot!

CHALK HORSE

Just like the Cerne Abbas Giant above, this horse has been carved into a chalky hill. It can be found in Cherhill in Wiltshire, and it dates back to the late 18th century.

19

During the summer, the countryside is very colourful. Poppies are used for medicines, rapeseed is harvested for its oil, and lavender is used by the perfume industry. See if you can smell the difference in the crops.

POPPY FIELD   Points: 15

Points: 15   **RAPESEED FIELD**

LAVENDER FIELD   Points: 15

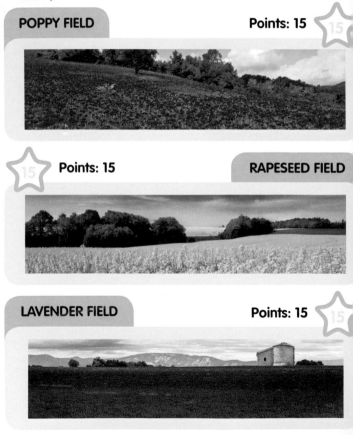

There are many animals in our countryside – here are just a few.

COWS

Points: 5

DEER

Points: 20

SHEEP

Points: 5
double with lambs

PIGS

Points: 5
double with piglets

HORSES

Points: 5

HIGHLAND CATTLE

Points: 20

CONVEX MIRROR

This convex mirror helps drivers see round corners on narrow roads by giving a wide angle.

Points: 20

BALES OF STRAW

Bales of straw fill the fields in May and June and change the appearance of the field.

Points: 10

TRACTOR

pio3 / shutterstock.com

After the harvest, tractors plough the fields ready for the next crop.

Points: 10

COMBINE HARVESTER

Giant combine harvesters gather in wheat.

Points: 15

TRUCK WITH CRANE

Heavy loads are carried on trucks that have small cranes which allow them to lift goods.

 Points: 20

TRUCK TRAILER

Articulated lorries transport huge containers.

Points: 5

FORK-LIFT TRUCK

Fork-lift trucks move pallets from warehouses to other trucks quickly and easily.

Points: 10

REFUSE COLLECTOR

ChameleonsEye / Shutterstock.com

Watch out for the bin lorry in your road!

Points: 5

TAXI

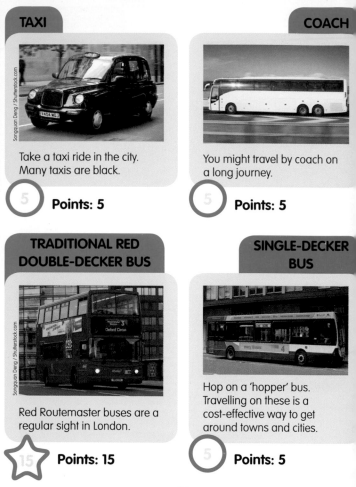

Songquan Deng / Shutterstock.com

Take a taxi ride in the city.
Many taxis are black.

Points: 5

COACH

You might travel by coach on
a long journey.

Points: 5

TRADITIONAL RED DOUBLE-DECKER BUS

Songquan Deng / Shutterstock.com

Red Routemaster buses are a
regular sight in London.

Points: 15

SINGLE-DECKER BUS

Hop on a 'hopper' bus.
Travelling on these is a
cost-effective way to get
around towns and cities.

Points: 5

DOUBLE-DECKER BUS (NOT RED)

Top Spot!   Points: 25

Double-decker buses have a great view from the top deck and older model buses in particular are often used for tourist trips.

CAR WITH BIKES

Points: 10 10

Look out for cars carrying bikes on the roof...

Points: 15 15

CAR WITH BOAT

...or even a canoe for the more adventurous!

CAR WITH ROOF BOX

Points: 5 5

Rooftop boxes can store everything you need for a holiday.

JuliusKielaitis / shutterstock.com

CYCLE COURIER
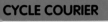

Cycle couriers are often quicker than courier vans in busy cities.

Points: 10

COURIER VAN

Delivering many small parcels every day.

Points: 5

CARAVAN

Caravans and camper vans let you pack up and take your home wherever you like!

Points: 5

CAMPER VAN

For ultimate mobility – with your own luxuries.

Points: 5

MILK FLOAT

Points: 5 5

Milk floats are driven by electric motors in the cities.

15 **Points: 15**

TRACTION ENGINE

Old steam-driven vehicles are often shown at fêtes – see if you can have a ride on one!

Jeff Dalton / shutterstock.com

STEAMROLLER

Points: 15 15

Thomas Owen Jenkins / shutterstock.com

Steamrollers are used to flatten road surfaces. The one shown in the photo, however, is being displayed at a fête.

CAR TRANSPORTER

New cars appear to be perched on top of car transporters but are safely tied down.

Points: 5

VINTAGE TRUCK

Karasev Victor / shutterstock.com

Old vintage trucks are rounder and slower than modern ones.

Points: 20

SNACK VAN

Snack vans generally have a serving hatch at the side, with a fold-out canopy.

Points: 5

ICE CREAM VAN

Lucian Milasan / Shutterstock.com

Or you might prefer something a bit colder!

Points: 5

POWER STATION

Giant concrete cooling towers puff out clouds of steam from power stations.

 **Points: 15**

PYLONS

The electricity generated by the power station is carried across the country on high wires held up by steel pylons.

Points: 5

WINDMILL

Windmills use the breeze to turn their sails.

 **Points: 15**

WIND TURBINES

Wind turbines use the wind to generate electricity.

Points: 5

WATERMILL

Top Spot!   **Points: 25**

Look out for an old-fashioned waterwheel turning water into power.

FUNFAIR

Points: 15

No one can resist the fun of the fair!

Points: 25   **Top Spot!**

MORRIS DANCING

A traditional style dating back hundreds of years. It is popular at village fêtes.

CRICKET

Points: 15

You may see a game being played on a village green, especially on a summer's day.

KITE FLYING

Take advantage of the sea breeze to fly a kite. Great fun!

Points: 15

LAWN BOWLS

Philip Bird LRPS CPAGB / shutterstock.com

Bowls is a skilful game, famously played by Sir Francis Drake in 1588!

Points: 15

UNICYCLE

Have fun on a one-wheel unicycle...

Points: 30 Top Spot!

TANDEM

gabriel12 / Shutterstock.com

...or on a bicycle made for two!

Points: 20

BY THE SEA

WHITE CLIFFS

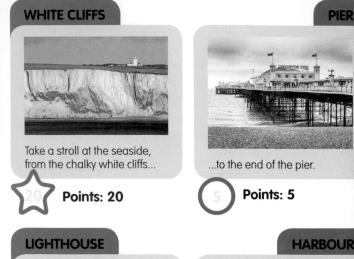

Take a stroll at the seaside, from the chalky white cliffs...

Points: 20

PIER

...to the end of the pier.

Points: 5

LIGHTHOUSE

Perhaps you can climb to the top of the lighthouse...

 Points: 15

HARBOUR

...or take a boat trip?

Points: 5

Points: 5

SAILING BOAT

Beginners learn to sail in small dinghies.

NARROW BOAT

Points: 5

Go for a stroll along a canal to see some colourful barges and long boats.

STARLING

Cheeky birds which gather at motorway service stations as they watch out for titbits from passing motorists.

 Points: 5

MAGPIE

A large black and white bird with a long tail. You will often see them feeding on roadkill.

Points: 5

BLACK-HEADED GULL

Flocks of gulls are often seen following the farmer's plough or at landfill sites.

Points: 5

ROOK

Flocks of these distinctive members of the crow family can often be seen feeding in roadside fields.

Points: 5

PHEASANT

Most often spotted strutting around verges and field boundaries. The males are more colourful than the females.

Points: 10

HOUSE SPARROW

Can be seen dust bathing at the side of the road or scavenging for crumbs under tables at roadside pubs.

Points: 5

BUZZARD

Buzzards are very large and can regularly be spotted from the car, circling in the sky or sitting on fence posts.

Points: 10

PIED WAGTAIL

Wagtails happily swap from countryside to urban life and back. They're as happy in the motorway services as in rivers and streams.

Points: 5

COMMON YEW

You are most likely to find yew trees growing in churchyards.

 Points: 5

COMMON ASH

Ash is used to make hammer and spade handles and is also popular with furniture makers.

Points: 5

BEECH

Easily found in spring: bluebells carpet their wizened roots.

 Points: 5

HORSE CHESTNUT

Best known for their autumn crop of nuts which children can use to play 'conkers' for hours.

 **Points: 5**

HAWTHORN

Commonly found as an impenetrable thorny hedge, ideal for containing animals.

Points: 5

BLACKTHORN

The fruit of the blackthorn is a small bitter plum or 'sloe', often used to make a tasty jam or sloe gin.

Points: 5

ELDER

The elder is small by tree standards – usually not much more than a bush.

Points: 5

SILVER BIRCH

Long associated with the start of new life due to its outstanding ability to colonise bare land after a forest is felled.

Points: 5

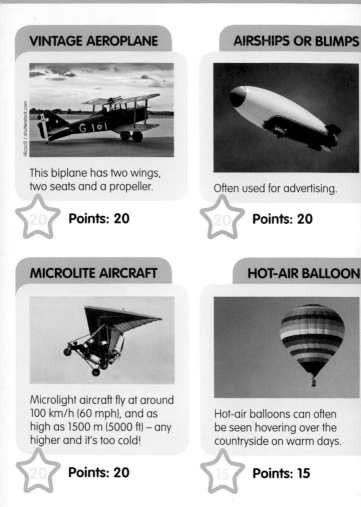

VINTAGE AEROPLANE

This biplane has two wings, two seats and a propeller.

Points: 20

AIRSHIPS OR BLIMPS

Often used for advertising.

Points: 20

MICROLITE AIRCRAFT

Microlight aircraft fly at around 100 km/h (60 mph), and as high as 1500 m (5000 ft) – any higher and it's too cold!

Points: 20

HOT-AIR BALLOON

Hot-air balloons can often be seen hovering over the countryside on warm days.

Points: 15

40

Points: 10

PLANE TAKING OFF

You will see planes taking off every couple of minutes from a busy airport.

GLIDER

Points: 20

Gliders are often towed into the sky by more powerful planes. They have no engine and use the wind and hot air to fly.

Points: 20

SKYDIVER

Experienced skydivers are able to land on a handkerchief!

41

LEVEL CROSSING

Points: 5 5

Stop at the level crossing to watch the train go by. Always be careful at level crossings.

Points: 20

STEAM TRAIN

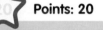

If you are lucky, you'll see an old steam train – just like the Hogwarts Express. Look for the steam coming out of the chimney.

FOOTBRIDGE

Points: 5 5

Stand on a footbridge and feel trains whizz past beneath your feet! Hold on to your hat!

Points: 10

ROAD AND RAIL BRIDGE

The road bridge in the foreground runs parallel to the old railway bridge.

WEIR

Weirs regulate the flow of water along a river.

Points: 20

CANAL LOCK

Locks on canals change the level of the water.

Points: 20

SUSPENSION BRIDGE

Points: 20

The Clifton Suspension Bridge in Bristol spans the River Avon, 75 m (245 ft) below. It was designed by the famous Victorian engineer I. K. Brunel (1806–1859).

20 MPH SPEED LIMIT

Usually by schools.

Points: 5

KEEP CLEAR

Points: 5

CYCLE LANE

Points: 5

SLOW

Points: 5
double if you can spot a
dual language sign

Watch out for these animal-related signs, particularly on roads passing through the countryside.

FROGS
Points: 15

HORSES
Points: 15

SHEEP
Points: 15

DEER
Points: 15

SQUIRRELS
Points: 15

DUCKS
Points: 15

UNEVEN ROAD

Points: 10

ROUNDABOUT

Points: 5

ONE WAY

Points: 5

NATIONAL SPEED

Maximum 70 mph.

Points: 5

NEW LAYOUT

Points: 10

ICE WARNING

Points: 10

TRACTORS TURNING

Tractors turning

Points: 10

LEVEL CROSSING

Points: 10

CHILDREN CROSSING

School

Points: 10

ELDERLY PEOPLE

Points: 10

BLIND SUMMIT

Points: 10

CONGESTION ZONE

Points: 5

BROWN ROAD SIGN

Points: 5

MOTORWAY SIGN

Points: 5

20 MPH SPEED LIMIT

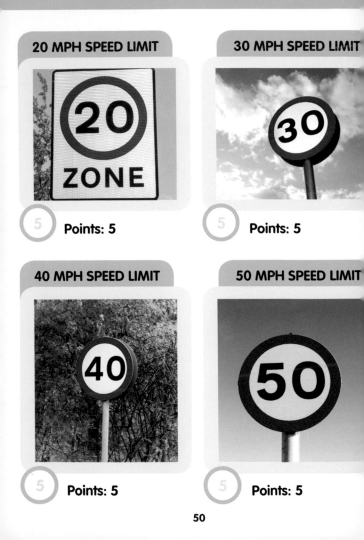

5 **Points: 5**

30 MPH SPEED LIMIT

5 **Points: 5**

40 MPH SPEED LIMIT

5 **Points: 5**

50 MPH SPEED LIMIT

5 **Points: 5**

Points: 10

OLD-FASHIONED ROAD SIGN

Old signs not only point you in the right direction, but the circular top tells you which district you're in!

ANCIENT ROAD SIGN

Points: 10

Before the 19th century, milestones let travellers know how far they had to walk or ride to their destination.

STATELY HOME

Points: 15
double if it is open to the public

Chatsworth House in Derbyshire is the home of the Duke and Duchess of Devonshire.

Points: 15

WATER TOWER

This brick water tower is topped by fancy crenellations.

TUDOR HOUSE

Points: 15

Black beams and white walls were common on 16th and 17th century houses.

Points: 20

OAST HOUSES

These were originally built as drying kilns for hops and malt. Mostly found in Kent.

DERELICT HOUSES

Points: 10

If you fancy something a little more comfortable, move on from this tumbledown house, to the grand entrance of a stately home.

Points: 10

STATELY HOME ENTRANCE

You might not be able to see stately homes from the car window because they are often set well back from the roadside. You may, however, be able to see an entrance with its grand gateposts.

CASTLE

Points: 10 10

Some castles are so big that you can see them from miles away. Keep an eye out on your car journey and you might be lucky enough to see one.

10 **Points: 10**

CASTLE RUINS

Some castles have crumbled over the years, while others have been well looked-after.

VIADUCT

Top Spot! **Points: 25** 25

Viaducts carry roads and railways across gorges. Look how many bricks were used to build this one!

There are many different companies supplying petrol and diesel to the millions of Britain's motorists. Garages are decorated in company colours and emblazoned with oil companies signs. Many garages double up as local convenience stores.

Points: 5

Points: 5

55

TEXACO

Attila JANDI / shutterstock.com

Points: 5
for any other petrol sign

MURCO

Points: 5
for any other petrol sign

SHELL

rnnoa357 / shutterstock.com

Points: 5
for any other petrol sign

TESCO

Barry Barnes / Shutterstock.com

Supermarkets sell around half of all of the fuel sold in the UK each year.

Points: 5
for any supermarket petrol sign

Places of worship are always worth looking at. You will find them in a number of styles, from ancient ruined buildings to modern structures that look quite unlike one another.

CHURCH

Points: 5

MOSQUE

Points: 10

Points: 10

MODERN CHURCH

Alastair Wallace / shutterstock.com

57

ABBEY

Points: 10

Coloured light pours in through beautiful stained glass windows.

 Points: 10

CATHEDRAL

Many cathedrals are decorated with amazing carved stone figures.

RUINED ABBEY

Points: 15

This abbey is now just a skeletal, roofless shell, but still interesting.

58

Many cities and towns have public clocks, as do churches and even some farms. Here are some to keep you ticking over.

FREESTANDING CLOCK TOWER

SUNDIAL

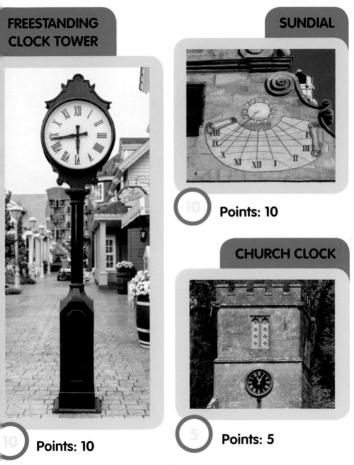

Points: 10

CHURCH CLOCK

Points: 5

Points: 10

STATION CLOCK

Points: 5 5

CLOCK ON SIDE OF BUILDING

10 **Points: 10**

MODERN CITY CLOCK

10 **Points: 10**

Points: 10

AIRPORT

You may be continuing your journey by plane.

TRAIN STATION

Points: 10

You may need to catch a train.

CAMPSITE

Perhaps your car journey will end at a campsite. Enjoy your holiday!

Points: 10

SEASIDE

Or you might be going for some fun at the seaside. Don't forget your bucket and spade!

Points: 10

INDEX

i-SPY

How to get your i-SPY certificate and badge

Let us know when you've become a Super-Spotter with 1000 point and we'll send you a special certificate and badge!

HERE'S WHAT TO DO!

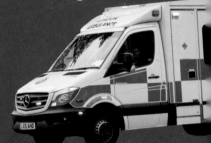

 Ask an adult to check your score.

Visit www.collins.co.uk/i-SPY to apply for your certificate. If you are under the age of 13 you will need a parent or guardian to do this.

We'll send your certificate via email and you'll receive a brilliant badge through the post!